The Bad
And The Good

Children's Sermons
And Activity Pages
For Lent And Easter

Julia E. Bland

CSS Publishing Company, Inc., Lima, Ohio

Dedicated to John

Scripture quotations are from the *New Revised Standard Version of the Bible*. copyright 1989 by the Division of Christian Education of the National Council of the Churches of Christ in the USA. Used by permission.

ISBN: 0-7880-0839-0

Table Of Contents

Introduction   4

Suggestions From The Author   4

Children's Sermons

    Lent 1: The Bad And The Good   5

    Lent 2: Push And Pull   6

    Lent 3: Sorrow And Joy   7

    Lent 4: Dirty And Clean   8

    Lent 5: Absent But Present   9

    Palm Sunday: Reject Or Accept   10

    Easter Sunday: Ugly And Beautiful   12

Children's Activity Pages   13

Answer Keys   27

Introduction

As the time for the suffering and death of Jesus approached, he began to tell his disciples the things that were to happen. Nearly every time he spoke of these events, he also gave them words of encouragement and hope. For instance, he would suffer and die **but** he would be raised on the third day (Matthew 20:18-19) and the disciples would know sorrow **but** the sorrow would turn to joy (John 16:20).

This series of Lenten sermons for children follows the example found in Jesus' teaching that the bad is followed by good, through trust in and obedience to the Heavenly Father.

Throughout this series, the children are asked to participate with word opposites. Because children like repetition, each sermon is begun in the same way, by letting them get involved in opposites.

The lessons are planned so that each child may take back to the pew an activity sheet. One side is a coloring page for young children. The other side has word puzzles and games for older children. The lessons are not limited to morning worship, however. They may be used any time there is opportunity for Christian education of children.

Suggestions From The Author

Study the sermon so that you can tell it in your own words using your own personality and with the needs of your local children in mind.

The sermon as given is to get you started. Be open to the Holy Spirit as he guides you to add your own personal observations.

If you need notes, make them small and tuck them inside your Bible at the page where you will be reading the Scripture.

Open the Bible and read from it. Children need to know that what you say really is from the Scriptures.

Ask questions and allow time for the children to answer. This will get them thinking and involved, but children can say unexpected things so be ready to guide them back to the subject.

Before the worship hour, clip the activity sheet, a pencil and crayons to a clipboard to be ready to hand to each child when the children's time is over.

As you pray and prepare, claim the Lord's promise in Isaiah 55:11:

> *So shall my word be that goes out from my mouth;*
> *it shall not return to me empty,*
> *but it shall accomplish that which I purpose,*
> *and succeed in the thing for which I sent it.*

Julia Bland

Lent 1: The Bad And The Good

Jesus was to die BUT he was to be raised to life.

Two Points: We know God loves us very much because Jesus died for us. With God's help, good things can follow bad things.

Scripture: Matthew 20:17-19 (NRSV)

Personal Background Devotions: Hebrews 5:7-9; Romans 5:5-8 (NRSV)

Visual Aid: A smooth or polished rock and one that is rough, or use driftwood and a piece of rough twig or limb.

Handouts: Activity sheets; smooth pebbles or driftwood, if available and desired.

Advance Preparations: Make copies of activity sheets, enough for each child to have one.

The Lesson:

Do you know what opposites are? If I say a word can you tell me the opposite? Let's try. What is the opposite of up? *(Give time for them to answer. Help them if necessary.)* What about big? (little). Black? (white). Night? (day). What about bad? (good). Let's stop and think about bad and good because those words remind me of something Jesus said. He was talking to his friends, the disciples, and he told them that something bad was going to happen. After the bad things, then there would be something good. Listen to Matthew 20:17-19:

> *While Jesus was going up to Jerusalem, he took the twelve disciples aside by themselves, and said to them on the way, "See, we are going up to Jerusalem, and the Son of Man* (that's Jesus) *will be handed over to the chief priests and scribes, and they will condemn him to death; then they will hand him over to the Gentiles to be mocked and flogged and crucified; and on the third day he will be raised."*

Jesus said that the powerful religious rulers were going to arrest him, make fun of him, hit and beat him, and then have him put on a cross to die.

This was a bad thing, a very bad thing.

But Jesus said that three days later he would be raised, he would come back to life. That was the good thing, a really good thing for Jesus *and* for us. One of the reasons that this is a good thing for us is because it proves how very much God loves us. But Jesus had to trust his Heavenly Father to take the bad things and make them good.

*Look at this beautiful polished rock (or driftwood). It is so smooth it almost feels soft. Why isn't it rough like this other one? They are opposites. One smooth and one rough. What has made the one smooth? It has been tumbled and rubbed, ground and polished in the movement and churning of the water where it once was (or perhaps in a rock polishing machine). All the rough edges are gone. We could say that the rubbing and tumbling and grinding was a bad thing, yet it has made the rock (wood) smooth and beautiful.

Something bad made something good.

Sometimes bad things happen to us. If we let our Heavenly Father help us learn, something good can follow. For instance: Suppose you fall and skin your knee. My! It hurts and it bleeds. Mom or Dad will help you clean all the dirt away and put on medicine and a BandAid. It is sore for several days. This was a bad thing to happen. How could something good follow? Because you know how badly it hurts, now you will be able to be sorry and help someone else when they have been hurt. Learning how to care, to be sorry, and to help others is the good thing that follows. We become a more beautiful person, not on the outside but inside where our feelings are. And this is God working in us to see that good is done.

The badness of the cross for Jesus was followed by the goodness of his being raised to life again, and because Jesus did this for us we know he loves us very much.

*Use visual aids

Lent 2: Push And Pull

Jesus was pushed onto a cross BUT the cross and his love pull us to him.

The Point: Love is the best way to live.

Scripture: John 12:27, 32-33 (NRSV)

Personal Background Devotions: Psalm 22:14-18, 27-31 (NRSV)

Visual Aid: A rough cross.

Handouts: Activity sheets; crosses, if you made them.

Advance Preparations: Copy enough activity sheets. To make a rough cross, use two small twigs or branches. Cross them and tie with thread or string. Make no attempt to make it attractive.

The Lesson:

If I say a word, can you tell me its opposite? Let's try. What is the opposite of rich? (poor). Of lost? (found). Down? (up). How about push? (pull). If you push someone, what are you doing? *(Show with hands.)* Are you moving or shoving them away from you? But if you pull someone, you move or bring them toward you. *(Show with hands.)* You might say that you draw them near you. Jesus told his friends that he was going to die. It was very hard for his friends to understand. They thought: If Jesus is really the Son of God, why does he have to die? Surely the real Son of God would get rid of all his enemies and take over and rule the nation. But no, Jesus said in John 12:27 as he prayed to his Heavenly Father:

> *... what should I say — "Father, save me from this hour? No, it is for this reason that I have come to this hour."*

The reason he came to earth was to die and there were those pushing him away, pushing him toward the cross. So Jesus prepared to die by being lifted up on a cross. He said:

> *"And I, when I am lifted up from the earth, will draw all people to myself." He said this to indicate the kind of death he was to die.*

We see beautiful polished crosses in jewelry and in church, but the real cross was ugly. *Here is one that is ugly. It is to remind us that his cross was ugly. Pushing Jesus away and onto a cross was a bad thing, but it was followed by something very good. Jesus said that on the cross he would draw, or pull, all people to himself. You and I and others are pulled to Jesus by his great love for us as he died there on the cross. Jesus knows that love is the mightiest force of all. More people know him and love him than ever would have if he had been a great king with a mighty army. For hundreds of years he has drawn or pulled people toward himself. Jesus was a Jewish man living in a tiny country, but people of all countries have worshiped him because he chose to die on the cross and be raised to life. Jesus is teaching us that love is the best way of all to live. He wants us to love — to love him and to love others.

*Use visual aid

6

Lent 3: Sorrow And Joy

The disciples would have sorrow BUT it would turn to joy.

The Point: Joy is promised to us if we love and obey Jesus.

Scripture: John 16:22; 15:10-11 (NRSV)

Personal Background Devotions: Hebrews 12:2 (NRSV)

Visual Aid: The sad/happy upside-down face from the activity sheet.

Handouts: Activity sheets; sunshine faces from the activity sheet, one for each child, if desired.

Advance Preparations: Make copies of the activity sheet. Cut out one of the upside-down faces from the activity sheet. If desired, color and mount on a heavier piece of paper.

The Lesson:

Are you all ready to tell me some opposites? What is the opposite of awake? (asleep). Hot? (cold). Happy? (sad). Have you ever been sad? Very sad? Did you cry? What makes us sad? Perhaps our dog or cat dies. Maybe there is a divorce in our family. Or perhaps someone we love very much dies. We are so sad that our insides feel like they are broken. Jesus knows how that feels. He was once so sad that he felt like he was broken. It was when those whom he loved hated him enough to kill him on the cross. We call this kind of sadness *sorrow.

Something Jesus told his disciples made them very sad. He told them several times that he was going to die and they would weep (cry) and mourn (be sad). It's a bad thing to be so sad. But Jesus said their sorrow and pain would turn to joy, that is, much happiness, because they would see him again.

> *"So you have pain now; but I will see you again, and your hearts will rejoice, and no one will take your joy from you."* — John 16:22

*Jesus said he would live again and they would have joy. That's a very good thing.

Jesus said we too can have joy. Our joy, our happiness, comes from knowing Jesus is alive and loving him and knowing he loves us. And then by doing what he says:

> *"If you keep my commandments, you will abide in my love, just as I have kept my Father's commandments and abide in his love. I have said these things to you so that my joy may be in you, and that your joy may be complete."* — John 15:10-11

When sad things happen, it helps to know that Jesus knows how it feels to be sad. We can pray and ask for help. In the middle of sadness we can have joy knowing Jesus loves us, understands, and will help if we trust him that he knows and does what is best.

*Use visual aid: First show the sad face, then turn upside-down for the happy face.

Lent 4: Dirty And Clean

We all have sin BUT we can be cleansed.

The Point: The blood of Jesus from the cross cleans away our sins.

Scripture: James 4:8; Matthew 26:28; 1 John 1:7, 9 (NRSV)

Personal Background Devotions: Psalms 24:3-6 (NRSV)

Visual Aid: A bar of soap.

Handouts: Activity sheets; little bars of soap, if desired.

Advance Preparations: Make copies of activity sheets.

The Lesson:

We've been talking about opposites. This time can you think of any to ask me? *(Let them work on this. Help if necessary.)* Does your mother ever look at your hands and say, "Oh my! Go wash!"? Do you have to wash before you eat? And maybe your hands don't even look dirty?

Did you know there might be dirt on your hands that you can't see? Dirt that we call germs and that can make you sick? These dirty germs get on our hands when we touch things that others touch, and then we put our fingers in our mouths, ears, or eyes. This especially happens when there are colds and flu around. *So you should wash with soap and wash often, even if you can't see any dirt.

The Bible tells us there is also another kind of dirt that we can't see. This dirt is sin. Sin starts at the heart and mind and spreads to the hands. God says we need to clean our hearts and hands.

A part of verse 8 of James 4 says:

> *Cleanse your hands, you sinners, and purify your hearts ...*

When we do wrong things, this is sin, and God says our hands look dirty to him. Even though we might not have used our hands to do the wrong thing, God says our hands look dirty. Do you ever talk back to your parents, say something to hurt someone, lie or cheat or perhaps push or grab? Well, there is a long list of things we all do that we shouldn't, and God sees it and says our hands are dirty. Sin is bad because it always hurts someone.

*What shall we do, because soap and water will not clean away this kind of dirt? This is a very bad thing.

Did you know that Jesus came to earth not only to teach us how to live, but also to die for us for the purpose of helping us get rid of sinful, dirty hearts and hands? In Matthew 26:28 he said:

> *... my blood ... is poured out for many for the forgiveness of sins.*

And this is a good thing, a wonderfully good thing.

Jesus said that his blood poured out as he died on the cross can get rid of dirty sins.

> *If we confess* (that means tell God we're sorry) *our sins, he who is faithful and just* (that means God) *will forgive us our sins and cleanse us from all unrighteousness.* (That means all the things we do that are wrong.)
> — 1 John 1:9

And in verse 7 we are told that it is the blood of Jesus that cleanses us. God uses Jesus' blood to wash away all our sins! We don't understand it, but we believe it, because the Bible says it's so. At night when we bathe or clean up before bed, if we can remember to pray, asking God to forgive us, then we can go to bed clean, both inside and out!

•Use visual aid

Lent 5: Absent But Present

Jesus was leaving BUT his spirit would be present.

The Point: Jesus sent the Holy Spirit to help all who love and obey him.

Scripture: John 16:7; 14:23 (NRSV)

Personal Background Devotions: John 14 (NRSV)

Visual Aid: Notebook or paper prepared to call the roll.

Handouts: Activity sheets; stickers to indicate "present" on their activity sheets, if desired.

Advance Preparations: Make copies of activity sheets. Prepare a list of names of children who usually attend. Have a pencil ready to add any children's names you might not have thought of or who might come unexpectedly. Make sure there is room to include all names. Leave no one out. Use this to call a roll.

The Lesson:

Let's see if we can think of some opposites again. What is the opposite of under? (over). Wet? (dry). Boy? (girl). How about absent? (present). What does it mean to be present? You are here. What does it mean to be absent? You are not here.

*Now I have here a list of boys and girls we usually see here on Sunday morning. I'll call the names and if you are here, say present. I'll make a P for present beside your name ... Are there names I have not called? I will write your name here on my list and put a P for present by your name, too. You are all present. Let's see if any are absent. *(Look at the list.)* Yes, here is _____ and _____ who are absent and we miss them **OR** no, everyone is present and that is great.

One day Jesus told his disciples that soon he would be absent. Soon he would die on the cross, to be raised to life, and then go home to heaven to be with his Father. The disciples were upset and sad. They had been present with Jesus, going place to place with him, listening to him teach for two or three years. They had hoped he would become king. Yet, here he was telling them that soon he would die, be raised to life, and leave them. He would be absent from them. This is a bad thing, a very bad thing, Jesus' leaving.

But Jesus said there is a good thing, a very good thing that will happen. As soon as he was home with his Father he would send his Holy Spirit. Jesus said in John 16:7:

> *"Nevertheless I tell you the truth: it is to your advantage that I go away, for if I do not go away, the Advocate* (Holy Spirit) *will not come to you; but if I go, I will send him to you."*

The Holy Spirit is Jesus and God the Father with us even though we don't see them. The Holy Spirit does not have to stay in one place at one time as did Jesus when he lived on earth. He can be everywhere with everyone who loves and obeys him. He was with the disciples then, and because he is spirit, he is also with us today and with people all around the world. Jesus as one person on the earth could not do that. This is a very good, happy thing. In John 14:23 Jesus said:

> *"Those who love me will keep my word, and my Father will love them, and we will come to them and make our home with them."*

He is here with us now to help, whether we are here or home or at school, with all that we do.

*Use visual aid

9

Palm Sunday: Reject Or Accept

Jesus was rejected BUT all who accept him become children of God.

The Point: All who accept Jesus and believe in him will become children of God.

Scripture: Luke 9:22; Mark 11:8-9; John 1:12 (NRSV)

Personal Background Devotions: Isaiah 53 (NRSV)

Visual Aid: One beautiful, red plastic apple and one yellow or green real apple, both in a sack.

Handouts: Activity sheets; apples, if desired.

Advance Preparations: Make copies of the activity sheets. Plastic apples can be bought in craft stores or where household decorations are sold.

The Lesson:

We've been talking about opposites. You know lots of opposites. What is the opposite of bad? (good). Big? (little). Up? (down). Sorrow? (joy). Absent? (present). Push? (pull). Here's a new one. Do you know the opposite of reject? This may be hard.

The opposite of reject is accept. What does it mean to accept something? It means we want it. We take it gladly. What does it mean to reject something? We don't want it. We won't take it.

Now, I think I'd like an apple. My idea of an apple is that it should be big, red and shiny. I would accept a big, red, shiny apple. *Maybe there is one in this sack. *(Pull out the green or yellow real one.)* What's this? An apple? It's not my idea of an apple. An apple should be big, red and shiny. I reject this yellow (green) one. I will look in the sack again. Ah! Here's what I'm looking for. I will accept this one.

I'm going to pass both apples around. Don't say a word, but you decide if I have rejected and accepted the right one. *(Pause as apples are passed around.)* Now, you've all looked at them, so what do you think? What? I have rejected the wrong one?

When Jesus taught, there were people who accepted him. They saw him heal people and teach and feed hungry people. They even saw him raise people from the dead. They listened and were willing to learn from him. They loved him, they believed he came from God, and they accepted him.

At the same time there were those who rejected him, because to them Jesus did not look like one sent from God. He was poor, not rich, and instead of making war on enemies, he taught love and forgiveness. He told them they were sinners; he didn't keep their rules. Those were things that they didn't like and wouldn't accept. This was a bad thing!

Today is called Palm Sunday and we think of those people who accepted Jesus as he came riding a donkey.

> *Many people spread their cloaks on the road, and others spread leafy branches that they had cut in the fields. Then those who went ahead and those who followed were shouting, "Hosanna! Blessed is the one who comes in the name of the Lord!"* — Mark 11:8-9

Aren't you glad there was a day when people accepted him and sang praises to him?

But at this same time those who rejected him were probably thinking like this: He comes riding into town on a peaceful, humble little donkey. If he were really the Son of God, he'd come to town on a big fine horse, making war on our enemies. He doesn't look or act like the Son of God should. The poor and common people are all who accept him and they know nothing at all! If we don't stop him now, they'll make him a king and we'll lose our job as their religious rulers.

And so it was just as Jesus had said:

"The Son of Man (that means Jesus) must undergo great suffering, and be rejected (emphasize rejected) by the elders, chief priests, and scribes, and be killed, and on the third day be raised." — Luke 9:22

Those rulers were wrong to reject him, the real Son of God, just as I was wrong when I rejected the real apple, just because it didn't look like I thought it should. Yet many people did and do accept Jesus as Lord, Son of God, and they love him by trying to do as he wants. For those that do, a wonderful good thing happens. They become children of God as promised in John 1:12:

But to all who received him (that means accept), *who believed in his name, he gave power to become children of God.*

I hope that each one of you will make up your minds to accept Jesus, sent from God to die for you and be raised on the third day, as your Lord. And that you will love him enough to do as he has said.

*Use visual aid

Easter Sunday: Ugly And Beautiful

Death is ugly BUT resurrection is beautiful.

The Point: Jesus promises that his people will live again just as he does.

Scripture: John 11:25b-26a (NRSV)

Personal Background Devotions: Matthew 27—28:10 (NRSV)

Visual Aid: Pearls, real or imitation. (These may be jewelry. Strings of imitation pearls for craft purposes can be found in craft departments of variety stores.)

Handouts: Activity sheets and, if desired, a pearl-decorated bookmark.

Advance Preparations: Copy enough activity sheets for the children. If desired, make bookmarks. Use tiny, simulated strung pearls, and glue or sew the pearls to heavy ribbon or strips of felt in the shape of a cross. Using plenty of glue and a toothpick to help apply them, set the pearls in the shape of a cross.

The Lesson:
You know what opposites are, don't you? Let's see if we can remember some that we've talked about. What is the opposite of bad? (good). Jesus showed us that God loves us and can turn bad things into good. What about push? (pull). Jesus was pushed onto a cross, but his great love pulls people to him. Sorrow? (joy). Jesus turned his friends' sorrow into joy when he rose from the dead, and he promises us joy, too, if we'll love and obey him. What about dirty? (clean). Jesus cleans away our sins with his blood. How about absent? (present). Jesus was leaving, but his Spirit is always present. What about reject? (accept). Some people did reject Jesus, but many have accepted him, and all who do become children of God. Wow! in every case, Jesus turns the bad into good.

Today, on Easter Sunday, I have one more word for you. What is the opposite of ugly? Yes, beautiful! I have something here that is beautiful. I have some pearls. *Do you know how real pearls are made? Pearls are made by small sea creatures called oysters. Oysters sit in one place at the bottom of the sea. They have a bottom shell and a top one. When they are hungry, they can lift the top one open and let bits of food drift in and get trapped inside the shell. Sometimes a small, sharp, ugly piece of sand will also get trapped inside the shell. The sand is ugly and painful. This is a bad thing to happen.

How does your foot feel when you get a rock in your shoe? Do you stop what you are doing and take it out? Of course. It is very painful and it could make a sore on your foot.

Well, the oyster has no way to remove the sand. The sand is sharp, ugly, and painful, so the oyster begins to surround it with layers and layers of a smooth, pearly stuff that the oyster can make, until it no longer is sharp and painful. And that is how a pearl is made. The pearl is a good and beautiful thing that came from something ugly and painful.

If there has been no ugly, painful death on the cross, there would be no beautiful resurrection for Jesus or for us. We never need to fear death, for Jesus said in John 11:25b-26a:

> ... *"I am the resurrection and the life. Those who believe in me, even though they die, will live, and everyone who lives and believes in me will never die."*

Dying is bad, but Jesus promises his people they will live again just like he does! This is what God's people celebrate on Easter Sunday, and that is good, very, very good!

*Use visual aid

WE WANT TO HELP SOMEONE
WHO IS HURT.

LENT 1: THE BAD AND THE GOOD

WHILE JESUS WAS GOING UP TO JERUSA-
LEM, HE TOOK THE TWELVE DISCIPLES
ASIDE BY THEMSELVES, AND SAID TO
THEM ON THE WAY, "SEE, WE ARE GOING
UP TO JERUSALEM, AND THE SON OF
MAN WILL BE HANDED OVER TO THE
CHIEF PRIESTS AND SCRIBES, AND THEY
WILL CONDEMN HIM TO DEATH; THEN
THEY WILL HAND HIM OVER TO THE
GENTILES TO BE MOCKED AND FLOGGED
AND CRUCIFIED; AND ON THE THIRD
DAY HE WILL BE RAISED."
MATTHEW 20:17-19

Find and circle words from the list. They go left to right or down.

```
k n e e b l o v e
a b s f a l l c d
e g o o d r o c k
c a r e r o u g h
h u r t l e a r n
f g y s m o o t h
```

good
bad
smooth
rough
fall
hurt
care
sorry
rock
learn
knee
love

What good thing did
Jesus say would happen
3 days after his death?

_____

**DRAW A LINE FROM ONE WORD
OR WORDS TO ITS MEANING. ONE
HAS BEEN DONE TO SHOW YOU HOW.
THESE WORDS ARE FOUND IN MATTHEW 20:17-19.**

Son of Man   religious rulers
twelve disciples   made fun
chief priests and scribes   hang from a cross until dead
mocked   beaten
flogged   Jesus
crucified   friends and followers of Jesus
raised   alive again

FILL IN THE BLANKS USING WORDS THAT RHYME.

A _ _ _ _ _ piece of wood that _ _ _ _ _ into a river will become
   tough   calls

smooth by being pushed with _ _ _ _ _ back and forth over the
                             saves

_ _ _ _ and pebbles of the river bed. A rough _ _ _ _ can be made
hand   sock

smooth in the same _ _ _. The rough treatment or trouble that the
                   day

_ _ _ _ _ or _ _ _ _ _ received has made it smooth and beautiful. If we
good   sock

love and trust Jesus to help, trouble can make us beautiful too.

_____

A piece of wood made smooth by water is called _ _ _ _ _ _ _ _ _ _ .
                                                 itfdroodw

**The crossword puzzle
goes across then
down.**

Jesus died on a
_____. So we
know how much God
_____ us.

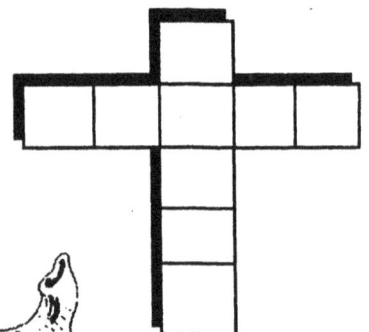

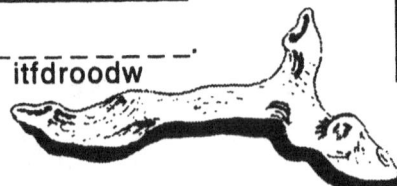

JESUS TEACHES ABOUT THE CROSS.

"AND I, WHEN I AM LIFTED UP FROM THE EARTH, WILL DRAW ALL PEOPLE TO MYSELF." HE SAID THIS TO INDICATE THE KIND OF DEATH HE WAS TO DIE. JOHN 12:32-33

The following words are found in John 12:32-33. Draw a line to match the word or words to what they mean.

lifted up	tell the detail
draw	Jesus
I	all kinds of people
all people	pull
indicate	hung on the cross

FILL IN THE BLANKS USING WORDS THAT ARE OPPOSITE OF THE ONE SHOWN UNDER THE LINES. SEE THE LIST.

He
pulls
death
good
bad
ugly
friends
die

Jesus knew he was going to _ _ _. His _ _ _ _ _ _ _ couldn't under-
  live   enemies

stand. The real cross was _ _ _ _. His death was _ _ _ but it was
  beautiful   good

followed by something _ _ _ _. His _ _ _ _ _ on a cross _ _ _ _ _
  bad   life   pushes

people to him. _ _ was willing to die because he loves us. Love is the
  she

mightiest force of all.

Work the crossword puzzle by going down then across.

Jesus draws _____ to himself with his love when he died on the _____.

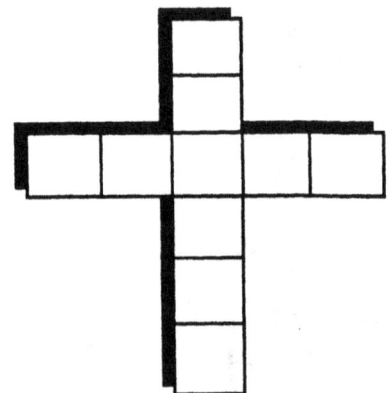

Jesus told his disciples,
"So you have pain now;
BUT (turn upside-down)

"I will see you again, and your hearts
will rejoice, and no one will take your
joy from you." John 16:22

JESUS KNOWS HOW IT FEELS TO
BE SAD. HE WANTS TO HELP.

17

LENT 3: SORROW AND JOY

"IF YOU KEEP MY COMMAND-MENTS, YOU WILL ABIDE IN MY LOVE, JUST AS I HAVE KEPT MY FATHER'S COMMANDMENTS AND ABIDE IN HIS LOVE. I HAVE SAID THESE THINGS TO YOU SO THAT MY JOY MAY BE IN YOU, AND THAT YOUR JOY MAY BE COMPLETE." JOHN 15:10-11

The following words are found in John 15:10-11. Match the word to what it means by drawing a line.

sorrow	live in
joy	cry
commandments	very happy
abide	very sad
weep	everything necessary
complete	things Jesus said
	we should or should not do

DRAW A LINE TO THE CORRECT FINISH FOR EACH SENTENCE.

Jesus knows how	Jesus will help.
Jesus loved those	see his disciples again.
Jesus said he would	it feels to be very sad.
Jesus promised joy	who put him on a cross.
When sad things happen	for those who love and keep his commandments.

Work the crossword puzzle by going down, then across.

The _____ of the disciples turned to _____.

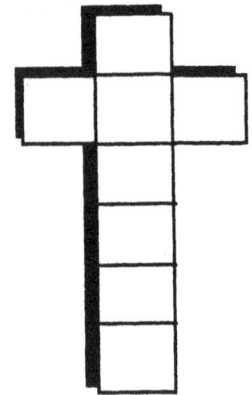

LOOK FOR WORDS THAT GO LEFT TO RIGHT OR DOWN. THEY ARE

_ _ p _ s _ _ e _.

alive	up
dead	down
happy	dirty
sad	clean
good	joy
bad	sorrow

```
a b s a d i r t y c d
a l i v e u c l e a n
b a d h a p p y j o y
e g o o d o w n f g h
i j k l s o r r o w m
```

COLOR THE SUNSHINE FACE YELLOW OR USE IT AS A PATTERN ON YELLOW CONSTRUCTION PAPER. CUT OUT THE CIRCLE. DRAW A SMILING FACE. CUT ON THE LINES. FOLD EVERY OTHER "SUN RAY" FORWARD. HANG WITH A STRING. IF YOU WANT, YOU CAN MAKE MORE THAN ONE. HANG THEM AS SHOWN.

IF WE TELL GOD WE ARE
SORRY, HE WILL FORGIVE US.

LENT 4: DIRTY AND CLEAN

IF WE CONFESS OUR SINS, HE WHO IS FAITHFUL AND JUST WILL FORGIVE US OUR SINS AND CLEANSE US FROM ALL UNRIGHTEOUSNESS ... THE BLOOD OF JESUS HIS SON CLEANSES US FROM ALL SIN. 1 JOHN 1:9, 7B

THE FOLLOWING WORDS ARE FOUND IN 1 JOHN 1:9, 7B. MATCH THE WORDS WITH THEIR MEANING BY DRAWING A LINE.

confess our sins

he who is faithful and just

cleanse

unrighteousness

sin

things we've done that are wrong

get rid of dirt or sin

things we've done that are wrong

God

tell God we're sorry

FILL IN THE MISSING WORDS. SEE THE LIST.

We should wash with s _ _ _ and water o _ _ _ _. We wash to c _ _ _ _ away

d _ _ _ and g _ _ _ _. We can't see germs but they can make us s _ _ _. God

says our h _ _ _ _ look dirty to him when we have done things we shouldn't.

These things are called sins. God will make us clean when we a _ _ him to. He

uses the b _ _ _ _ of Jesus.

ask
blood
sick
germs
soap
clean
often
dirt
hands

UNSCRAMBLE THE SENTENCE.

dirt rid Washing gets germs of and

_____ ___ ___ ___

___ _____ ___ ___ ■

Crossword Puzzle

Down:
Jesus was put on a
_____.

Across:
His _____ cleans away our sins.

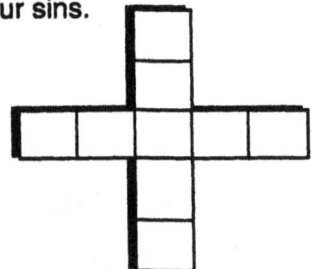

20

←SCHOOL

JESUS HELPS US.

LENT 5: ABSENT BUT PRESENT

"NEVERTHELESS I TELL YOU THE TRUTH: IT IS TO YOUR ADVANTAGE THAT I GO AWAY, FOR IF I DO NOT GO AWAY, THE ADVOCATE WILL NOT COME TO YOU; BUT IF I GO, I WILL SEND HIM TO YOU." JOHN 16:7

The following words are found in John 16:7.

Draw a line to match the word or words to what they mean.

advantage   God's Spirit who helps

I go away   to be better than before

Advocate   Jesus goes to be with God
                    the Father

FILL IN THE MISSING WORDS. SEE THE LIST.

Jesus told his disciples that soon he would be _ _ _ _ _ _. He would

_ _ _ on the cross to be raised to _ _ _ _ and then go _ _ _ _ to be

with his Father. The disciples were _ _ _. They had been _ _ _ _ _ _ _

with Jesus going place to place, listening to him teach for two or three

years. They had hoped he would become a king. Yet, here he was

telling them that soon he would die, be raised to life, and _ _ _ _ _

them. But Jesus said there is a _ _ _ _ thing that will happen. As soon

as he was home with his Father, he would send his _ _ _ _ _ _ _ _ _ _.

Even though we do not _ _ _ him, the Holy Spirit is with us to _ _ _ _.

good
leave
absent
life
die
home
Holy Spirit
see
help
sad
present

FIND THE WORDS. THEY GO LEFT TO RIGHT OR DOWN. SEE THE LIST.

```
h  e  l  p  a  b  c  l
e  d  e  r  g  h  i  e
l  i  f  e  j  k  l  a
p  a  b  s  e  n  t  v
m  g  h  e  r  e  n  e
s  o  o  n  d  i  e  l
e  o  m  t  o  p  r  o
n  d  e  o  b  e  y  v
d  i  s  c  i  p  l  e
```

present
absent
life
here
good
soon
go
home
help (two times)
die
obey
send
disciple
love
leave

My name is _____
I am present.

Work the crossword puzzle by going down, then across.

Jesus said he would be

_____,

but he would send the Holy Spirit to be _____.

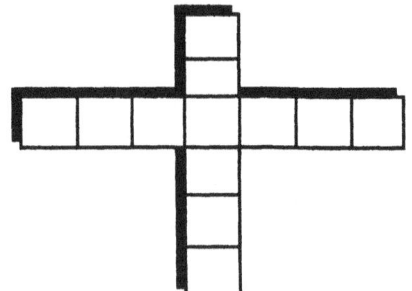

22

MANY PEOPLE ACCEPTED JESUS.
SOME REJECTED HIM.

PALM SUNDAY: ACCEPT OR REJECT

BUT TO ALL WHO RECEIVED HIM, WHO BELIEVED IN HIS NAME, HE GAVE POWER TO BECOME CHILDREN OF GOD. JOHN 1:12

The following words are found in John 1:12. Match the word or words to their meaning by drawing a line.

all	accepted him as Lord
received	know he came from God
believed in his name	everyone
power	God's family
children	ability

FILL IN THE BLANKS USING MARK 11:8-9 (NRSV) OR SEE THE LIST.

shouting
ahead
branches
cloaks
people
spread
fields
followed
Lord
one

Many _ _ _ _ _ _ spread their _ _ _ _ _ _ on the road, and others _ _ _ _ _ _

leafy _ _ _ _ _ _ _ _ that they had cut in the _ _ _ _ _ _. Then those who went

_ _ _ _ _ and those who _ _ _ _ _ _ _ _ were _ _ _ _ _ _ _ _ Hosanna! Blessed

is the _ _ _ who comes in the name of the _ _ _ _!

Work the crossword puzzle by going down, then across.

Some people _____ Jesus, but all who _____ him become children of God.

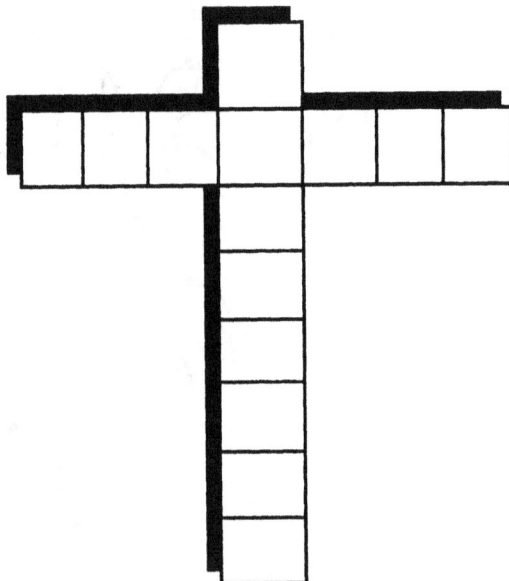

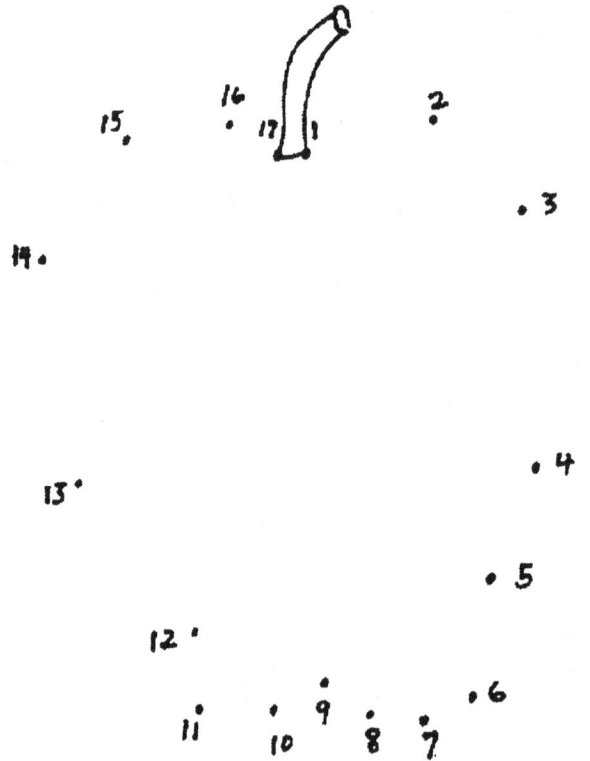

JESUS IS ALIVE.

EASTER SUNDAY: UGLY AND BEAUTIFUL

> "I AM THE RESURRECTION AND THE LIFE. THOSE WHO BELIEVE IN ME, EVEN THOUGH THEY DIE, WILL LIVE, AND EVERYONE WHO LIVES AND BELIEVES IN ME WILL NEVER DIE."
> JOHN 11:25B-26A

The following words are found in John 11:25b-26a. Match the words with what they mean by drawing a line.

I am   live forever
resurrection   accept Jesus as Lord
believe in me   a return to life
never die   Jesus

Oysters are little sea animals. When they are new, they are about as big as the point of a needle. They move around in the water while they are young. When they are old enough, they fasten themselves to a rock and stay there the rest of their lives. They have a bottom shell and a top shell with a hinge at one end, so that they can open to eat or close if they sense danger. Their shell protects them. Some oysters are called pearl oysters. If a tiny, painful grain of sand or other matter gets in their shell, they make layers of pearly stuff around it. Oysters make our beautiful, valuable pearls. Cultured pearls are made by oysters, too. They are in oyster farms where people put the sand into the shell. We can learn something from pearl oysters.

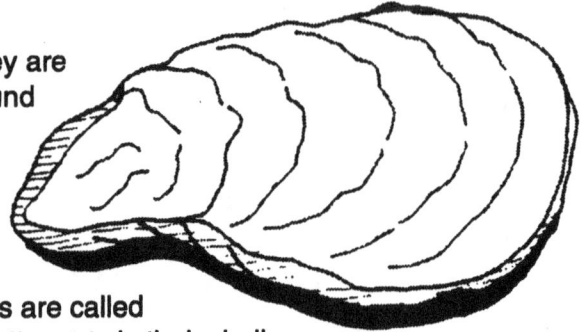

IF THERE WERE NO UGLY, PAINFUL PIECE OF SAND ...
There would be no pearls.

IF THERE HADN'T BEEN AN UGLY, PAINFUL DEATH ON THE CROSS ...
There would be no resurrection for Jesus or for us.

SOMETIMES TROUBLE THAT IS BAD, UGLY, OR PAINFUL MAKES "PEARLS" IN OUR LIVES.

Choose from the list some good things trouble might help us learn. Write them inside the pearls.
Trouble can make "pearls" in our life, if we love God and want his will done.
OR
Trouble can make us mad, bitter, hateful people if we do not love God nor want his will done ... We make the choice.

pray more
hate
trust God
mad
patience
be thankful
forgive others' failures
bitter

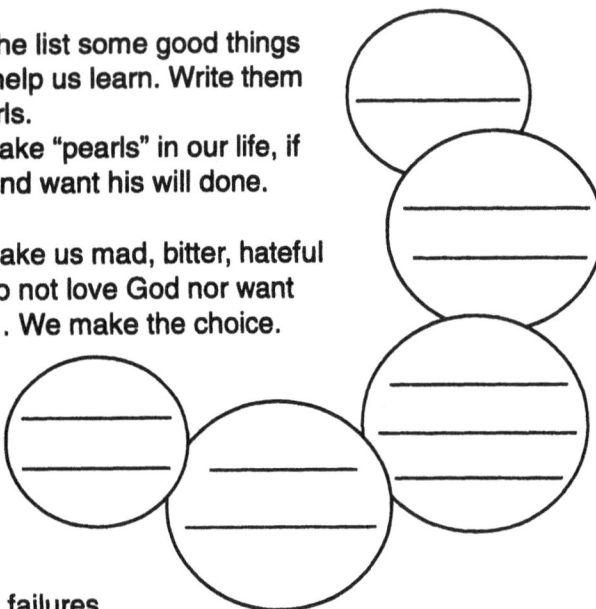

Crossword Puzzle

Across:
The _____ of Jesus on a cross was ugly.
Down:
Resurrection for Jesus and for us is _____.

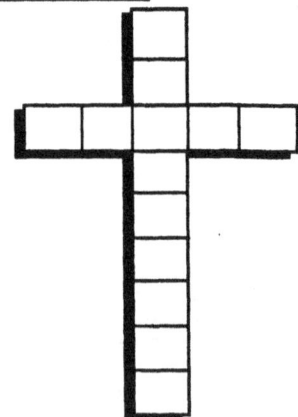

ANSWER KEYS
FOR
ACTIVITY
PAGES

WHILE JESUS WAS GOING UP TO JERUSALEM, HE TOOK THE TWELVE DISCIPLES ASIDE BY THEMSELVES, AND SAID TO THEM ON THE WAY, "SEE, WE ARE GOING UP TO JERUSALEM, AND THE SON OF MAN WILL BE HANDED OVER TO THE CHIEF PRIESTS AND SCRIBES, AND THEY WILL CONDEMN HIM TO DEATH; THEN THEY WILL HAND HIM OVER TO THE GENTILES TO BE MOCKED AND FLOGGED AND CRUCIFIED; AND ON THE THIRD DAY HE WILL BE RAISED."
MATTHEW 20:17-19

Find and circle words from the list. They go left to right or down.

good
bad
smooth
rough
tall
hurt
care
sorry
rock
learn
knee
love

What good thing did Jesus say would happen 3 days after his death?
he will be raised

DRAW A LINE FROM ONE WORD OR WORDS TO ITS MEANING. ONE HAS BEEN DONE TO SHOW YOU HOW. THESE WORDS ARE FOUND IN MATTHEW 20:17-19.

Son of Man — religious rulers
twelve disciples — made fun
chief priests and scribes — hang from a cross until dead
mocked — beaten
flogged — Jesus
crucified — friends and followers of Jesus
raised — alive again

FILL IN THE BLANKS USING WORDS THAT RHYME.

A **rough** piece of wood that **falls** into a river will become
(tough) (calls)

smooth by being pushed with **waves** back and forth over the
(saves)

sand and pebbles of the river bed. A rough **rock** can be made
(hand) (sock)

smooth in the same **way**. The rough treatment or trouble that the
(day)

wood or **rock** received has made it smooth and beautiful. If we
(good) (sock)

love and trust Jesus to help, trouble can make us beautiful too.

A piece of wood made smooth by water is called **driftwood**

The crossword puzzle goes across then down.

Jesus died on a **cross**. So we know how much God **loves** us

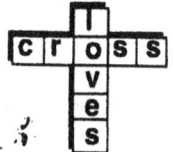

```
c r o s s
    o
    v
    e
    s
```

"I AM THE RESURRECTION AND THE LIFE. THOSE WHO BELIEVE IN ME, EVEN THOUGH THEY DIE, WILL LIVE, AND EVERYONE WHO LIVES AND BELIEVES IN ME WILL NEVER DIE."
JOHN 11:25B-26A

The following words are found in John 11:25b-26a. Match the words with what they mean by drawing a line.

I am — live forever
resurrection — accept Jesus as Lord
believe in me — a return to life
never die — Jesus

Oysters are little sea animals. When they are new they are about as big as the point of a needle. They move around in the water while they are young. When they are old enough, they fasten themselves to a rock and stay there the rest of their lives. They have a bottom shell and a top shell with a hinge at one end, so that they can open to eat or close if they sense danger. Their shell protects them. Some oysters are called pearl oysters. If a tiny, painful grain of sand or other matter gets in their shell they make layers of pearly stuff around it. Oysters make our beautiful, valuable pearls. Cultured pearls are made by oysters, too. They are in oyster farms where people put the sand into the shell. We can learn something from pearl oysters.

IF THERE WERE NO UGLY, PAINFUL PIECE OF SAND ...
There would be no pearls.

IF THERE HADN'T BEEN AN UGLY, PAINFUL DEATH ON THE CROSS ...
There would be no resurrection for Jesus or for us.

SOMETIMES TROUBLE THAT IS BAD, UGLY, OR PAINFUL MAKES "PEARLS" IN OUR LIVES.

Choose from the list some good things trouble might help us learn. Write them inside the pearls.
Trouble can make "pearls" in our life if we love God and want his will done
OR
Trouble can make us mad, bitter, hateful people if we do not love God nor want his will done. We make the choice.

pray more
hate
trust God
mad
patience
be thankful
forgive others' failures
bitter

(pearls: patience, trust God, forgive others failures, be thankful, pray more)

Crossword Puzzle
Across:
The __death__ of Jesus on a cross was ugly.
Down:
Resurrection for Jesus and for us is __beautiful__

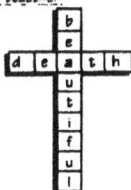

```
      b
      e
      a
d e a t h
      t
      i
      f
      u
      l
```

"NEVERTHELESS I TELL YOU THE TRUTH; IT IS TO YOUR ADVANTAGE THAT I GO AWAY, FOR IF I DO NOT GO AWAY, THE ADVOCATE WILL NOT COME TO YOU; BUT IF I GO, I WILL SEND HIM TO YOU." JOHN 16:7

The following words are found in John 16:7. Draw a line to match the word or words to what they mean.

advantage — God's Spirit who helps
I go away — to be better than before
Advocate — Jesus goes to be with God the Father

FILL IN THE MISSING WORDS. SEE THE LIST.

Jesus told his disciples that soon he would be **absent**. He would **die** on the cross to be raised to **life** and then go **home** to be with his Father. The disciples were **sad**. They had been **present** with Jesus going place to place, listening to him teach for two or three years. They had hoped he would become a king. Yet, here he was telling them that soon he would die, be raised to life, and **leave** them. But Jesus said there is a **good** thing that will happen. As soon as he was home with his Father, he would send his **Holy Spirit**. Even though we do not **see** him, the Holy Spirit is with us to **help**.

good
leave
absent
life
die
home
Holy Spirit
see
help
sad
present

FIND THE WORDS. THEY GO LEFT TO RIGHT OR DOWN. SEE THE LIST.

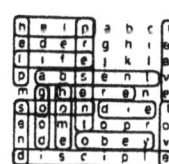

present
absent
life
here
good
soon
go
home
help (two times)
die
obey
send
disciple
love
leave

My name is
I am present.

Work the crossword puzzle by going down, then across.

Jesus said he would be **absent** but he would send the Holy Spirit to be **present**.

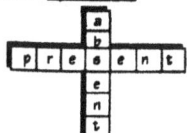

```
      a
      b
      s
p r e s e n t
      n
      t
```

Top Left

"AND I, WHEN I AM LIFTED UP FROM THE EARTH, WILL DRAW ALL PEOPLE TO MYSELF." HE SAID THIS TO INDICATE THE KIND OF DEATH HE WAS TO DIE. JOHN 12:32-33

The following words are found in John 12:32-33. Draw a line to match the word or words to what they mean.

lifted up — tell the detail
draw — Jesus
I — all kinds of people
all people — pull
indicate — hung on the cross

FILL IN THE BLANKS USING WORDS THAT ARE OPPOSITE OF THE ONE SHOWN UNDER THE LINES. SEE THE LIST.

Jesus knew he was going to d i e. (live) His f r i e n d s (enemies) couldn't understand. The real cross was u g l y (beautiful). His death was b a d (good) but it was followed by something g o o d (bad). His d e a t h (life) on a cross p u l l s (pushes) people to him. He (she) was willing to die because he loves us. Love is the mightiest force of all.

List: He, pulls, death, good, bad, ugly, friends, die

Work the crossword puzzle by going down then across.

Jesus draws __people__ to himself with his love when he died on the __cross__.

people
c r o s s
(cross / people)

Top Right

"IF YOU KEEP MY COMMANDMENTS, YOU WILL ABIDE IN MY LOVE, JUST AS I HAVE KEPT MY FATHER'S COMMANDMENTS AND ABIDE IN HIS LOVE. I HAVE SAID THESE THINGS TO YOU SO THAT MY JOY MAY BE IN YOU, AND THAT YOUR JOY MAY BE COMPLETE." JOHN 15:10-11

The following words are found in John 15:10-11. Match the word to what it means by drawing a line.

sorrow — live in
joy — cry
commandments — very sad
abide — very happy
weep — everything necessary
complete — things Jesus said we should or should not do

DRAW A LINE TO THE CORRECT FINISH FOR EACH SENTENCE.

Jesus knows how — Jesus will help
Jesus loved those — see his disciples again
Jesus said he would — it feels to be very sad
Jesus promised joy — who put him on a cross
When sad things happen — for those who love and keep his commandments

LOOK FOR WORDS THAT GO LEFT TO RIGHT OR DOWN. THEY ARE o p p o s i t e s.

alive — up
dead — down
happy — dirty
sad — clean
good — joy
bad — sorrow

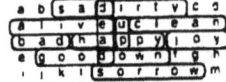

Work the crossword puzzle by going down, then across.

The __sorrow__ of the disciples turned to __joy__.

j o y
sorrow
(sorrow / joy)

COLOR THE SUNSHINE FACE YELLOW OR USE IT AS A PATTERN ON YELLOW CONSTRUCTION PAPER. CUT OUT THE CIRCLE. DRAW A SMILING FACE. CUT ON THE LINES. FOLD EVERY OTHER "SUN RAY" FORWARD. HANG WITH A STRING. IF YOU WANT, YOU CAN MAKE MORE THAN ONE. HANG THEM AS SHOWN.

Bottom Left

IF WE CONFESS OUR SINS, HE WHO IS FAITHFUL AND JUST WILL FORGIVE US OUR SINS AND CLEANSE US FROM ALL UNRIGHTEOUSNESS ... THE BLOOD OF JESUS HIS SON CLEANSES US FROM ALL SIN. 1 JOHN 1:9, 7B

THE FOLLOWING WORDS ARE FOUND IN 1 JOHN 1:9, 7B. MATCH THE WORDS WITH THEIR MEANING BY DRAWING A LINE.

confess our sins — things we've done that are wrong
he who is faithful and just — get rid of dirt or sin
cleanse — things we've done that are wrong
unrighteousness — God
sin — tell God we're sorry

FILL IN THE MISSING WORDS. SEE THE LIST.

We should wash with s o a p and water o f t e n. We wash to c l e a n away d i r t and g e r m s. We can't see germs but they can make us s i c k. God says our h a n d s look dirty to him when we have done things we shouldn't. These things are called sins. God will make us clean when we a s k him to. He uses the b l o o d of Jesus.

List: ask, blood, sick, germs, soap, clean, often, dirt, hands

UNSCRAMBLE THE SENTENCE.

dirt rid Washing gets germs of and
W a s h i n g   g e t s   r i d   o f   d i r t   a n d   g e r m s

Crossword Puzzle
Down: Jesus was put on a __cross__.
Across: His __blood__ cleans away our sins.

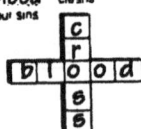

b l o o d / cross

Bottom Right

BUT TO ALL WHO RECEIVED HIM, WHO BELIEVED IN HIS NAME, HE GAVE POWER TO BECOME CHILDREN OF GOD. JOHN 1:12

The following words are found in John 1:12. Match the word or words to their meaning by drawing a line.

all — accepted him as Lord
received — know he came from God
believed in his name — everyone
power — God's family
children — ability

FILL IN THE BLANKS USING MARK 11:8-9 (NRSV) OR SEE THE LIST.

Many p e o p l e spread their c l o a k s on the road, and others s p r e a d leafy b r a n c h e s that they had cut in the f i e l d s. Then those who went a h e a d and those who f o l l o w e d were s h o u t i n g "Hosanna! Blessed is the o n e who comes in the name of the L o r d!"

List: shouting, ahead, branches, cloaks, people, spread, fields, followed, Lord, one

Work the crossword puzzle by going down, then across.

Some people __rejected__ Jesus, but all who __receive__ him become children of God.

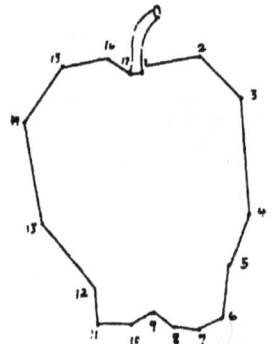

r e c e i v e
r e j e c t e d